CW00594910

BIRTHDAY PARTY

games – food – invitations – party bags

TRACEY BENTON

www.ziegel.co.uk

 ZIEGEL

Committed to environmentally responsible publishing.

Proudly Published in Devon in 2007 by Ziegel Publishing
36a Church Street, Braunton, Devon, EX33 2EL
editor@ziegel.co.uk
www.ziegel.co.uk

copyright © Ziegel Publishing 2007

Author & Editor: Tracey Benton
Photography & Design: Chris Dyer
Nutrition & Recipes: Hazel Radford
Proofreading: Mary Lu Hick
Sense Checking: Sandra Brain & Marianne Davies

A catalogue record for this book is available from the British Library
ISBN 978-0-9555144-0-1

OUR PUBLISHING PHILOSOPHY

This book is produced in Devon, it's where we live. Our policy is to make use of locally available talent and resources including printing and binding. This reduces our carbon emissions and therefore our impact on the environment. This book is also printed on 100% recycled paper using vegetable-based inks and a bio-degradable laminate on the cover.

TRACEY BENTON

This book is years of my personal experience distilled into a practical guide for other parents. All the games are really easy to play yet fantastic fun. I've chosen the firm favourites and, while they are intended for 4-11 year-olds, it has been known (on several occasions) for mums and dads to join in too. I hope these ideas give you and your family hours of fun.

CHRIS DYER

I didn't want to stage the photographs for this book, instead I captured children enjoying themselves in all their silly, noisy, blurred glory. I wanted to show children playing games in everyday environments - the village hall, a garden, or front room. After all that's where you'll be running your parties. As for the food, I've portrayed it just as it should be: home-made, simple and delicious.

HAZEL RADFORD

It's tempting to want to make heaps of beautifully presented food for your child's special day. The practicality is that even if you're fairly accomplished in the kitchen, you still need hours of preparation. As a mum I wanted to share with you my recipes for simple, tasty, natural food that children will actually eat.

CONTENTS

INTRODUCTION

Kids are great. Left to their own devices they can make anything fun. Do you remember the magic and endless possibilities of an empty box? Or the sheer joy of building a den with a few chairs and an old sheet? Those were the days.

Recently, I was in a room with my daughter Ellie and two boys of a friend. It was the first time they'd met and so all were a bit shy: one of the boys stuffed a cushion up his jumper. Naturally, the others followed suit thinking it was a great idea. That was it, rolling around, giggles and laughter for the next hour as they all pretended to be sumo wrestlers. Fabulously simple fun.

That's what I've tried to capture with the games in this book. Good old-fashioned, innocent, creative, energetic fun... with a modern twist. Don't spend a fortune, it's not necessary. Just make use of bits and bobs that you already have around the home. It's certainly the most fun you'll ever have with a plastic bucket and a few old socks.

I also asked nutritionist Hazel Radford to put together some simple party food suggestions. She's a mum and knows, from experience, that the last thing you want is to be slaving over elaborate food only to find that the kids won't eat it. At the same time sugared up kids are hard to handle so we are offering sensible alternatives to jam sandwiches, fizzy pop and mountains of sweets. I think she's done a fantastic job and hope everyone enjoys her recipes.

Tracey Benton

YOU CAN RUN THIS KIND OF PARTY ANYWHERE

You can run it in your front room, in the garden, as a picnic party in the local park, hire the village hall or, if you're lucky enough to live by the coast, it can be a beach party.

I'm not going to pretend that organising and running a children's birthday party is a relaxing project. That would be a fib. The main trick is not to get worked up about everything being perfect. That's missing the point entirely. It's a party, everyone should be enjoying themselves and anyway, it is only for a couple of hours. Just keep it simple – they'll have a great time and you'll stay relatively sane.

Remember, nobody is judging you, least of all the children. Other parents aren't either. In fact they're delighted that a) it's you entertaining the kids, not them and b) they've got a couple of hours of blissful peace and quiet.

HOW TO USE THIS BOOK

We've kept this book as easy to use as possible so that preparation, cost, fuss and stress are all kept to a minimum. We want you to enjoy the party as much (or at least 'almost' as much) as the children. The book is designed so that you can follow it page by page or, if you prefer, pick out the bits you like and do it your own way.

To keep it simple, the games are organised in a specific sequence. They are suitable for ages 4-11 and are all great fun yet really, really easy to play. They are quick to set up and there are no complicated rules to explain. All you have to do is choose which props you are going to use for each game and have them prepared in advance (make use of the handy checklist in this book). You may want to choose props that make the game harder for older children and easier for the younger ones. When you're ready to start with the fun and merriment, just follow the instructions page by page. It's as simple as that.

There are enough games to entertain a group of children for a standard 2 hour birthday party. Of course, the more children you have, the longer each game will take and vice versa. Most of the games are team games but they can be played with individual children competing against each other too - so it doesn't really matter how many children turn up on the day.

I've included additional games, just in case you have time to spare or if you are feeling brave enough to run a longer party.

For each game, you are given suggestions for any number of different props, some sillier than others. If you don't have any of these, just improvise. Use your imagination, there is sure to be something in the house you can use. If you're in a rush though, you can pick up any missing bits and bobs very cheaply from the local shops.

Why not use the party invitations to get each of the children to bring along a prop – they'll have fun trying to work out how on earth it will be used in the party.

PARTY POLITICS

HOW MANY KIDS TO INVITE?

That depends on how many you can handle. Seriously! Be sensible, recognise your limitations and don't try to compete with other parents. If you can only manage four kids, only invite four. Also think about how many people are willing to help you and how much space you've got. You can run the games in this book with anything from two children to the whole class. I tend to stick to around 8 children in total. I did invite the whole class once. Once was enough – I'll never do that again. Aim for even numbers but don't panic if the right number doesn't turn up. It's really not a problem.

POLITICS

Don't get caught up in petty playground politics; it's far too exhausting and can do more harm than good. If little Johnny or Jenny has fallen out with their best friend, the likelihood is that they'll be bosom buddies a week later. You'll know if the fall out is serious enough to exclude someone. (Other than instances of bullying, it rarely is.) At the same time don't pressurise your child into inviting someone they simply don't get on with. It is their special day after all. A tough balance, but use your judgement and don't get caught up in the politics of it all – life's too short.

PARTY BAGS

Don't feel bad if you don't send the children home with party bags full of loot. They usually go straight in the bin when they get home anyway. That's just a waste of money and effort. It's not exactly good for the environment either – all that plastic that won't decompose. Don't forget you're providing these children with two hours of fantastic fun and games. Surely that's more than enough? For Ellie's last party I just sent them home with a slice of birthday cake and nobody complained. Well, not to me anyway! If you do want to provide party bags, we have some great ideas for low-cost home-made options in this book.

THE PARTY BASICS

INVITATIONS
If you have time, make your own invitations with the birthday boy or girl. We have some simple ideas in this book that you might like to try – we've even got one you can photocopy or download from our website. How easy is that? You can also pick up cheap and cheerful invitations from the supermarket or local stationers. Try to send out your invitations about three weeks before the party date. Ring round a few days before the party just to check final numbers. Don't forget you can use the invitations to ask children to bring props for the party games.

THEMES
Don't be afraid of gearing the party around a theme. With a little imagination you can adapt any of the games to your chosen theme. We've made a few suggestions for you, just to get your creative juices flowing.

DECORATIONS
This is down to budget and personal choice. I used to go to loads of trouble but have found that it doesn't make any difference to the enjoyment of the party and only creates unnecessary waste. I now prefer loads of balloons scattered about the place. A few tied together and stuck to the walls makes the place look cheerful. Use masking tape to avoid damage. Tie a few streamers to the balloons to add a bit more colour. Cheap, simple and effective. Even better, you can also use the balloons in the games so they don't go to waste.

HOW TO RUN A STANDARD TWO HOUR PARTY

HERE'S HOW I WOULD ORGANISE THINGS

Welcome

Quick warm-up game to get everyone in the mood (5 minutes)

Games (40 minutes)

Comfort break (5 minutes)

More games (20 minutes)

Food (20 minutes)

Birthday cake & Happy Birthday sing-song (5 minutes)

Cool Down Games (15 minutes)

Final game while waiting for parents to arrive (10 minutes)

Goodbyes

Don't worry you don't even have to remember any of this.
Let this book lead the way for you, one page at a time. As
you've completed each game, just turn to the next page.
It's as simple as that.

DISTRACTION TACTICS

It only takes a minute or two to clear away the last game and set up the next. In other words, no time at all. But kids are kids. And frankly some are more boisterous than others. So I've included some simple distraction tactics to keep them occupied during that time, just in case.

Why not nominate a couple of children to help you set up each new game? Pick different children for each game. They can help set out the table for food too!

CHECKLIST

Use this to make a note of which props you will use for each game. You can use this the day before the party to double check that you have everything.

If you have asked children to bring props along, be aware that some of them might forget; so, have some spare just in case.

Game	The props you have already	Bits left to buy
Cloakroom Chaos		
Straws and Pretzels		
Squeezy Cheese and Crackers		
More Straws!		
Chopsticks		
Socks and Stuff		
Lemon Relay		
Balloon Games		
Pass the Parcel	Don't forget the string	
Musical Chairs	Don't forget the music	Don't forget the small gift for the centre.
That Chocolate Game		Don't forget a bar of good quality chocolate

OTHER ESSENTIALS

It's worth having a ball of string, a pile of newspapers and a roll of sticky tape handy in case you need to make some props.

Whatever you do: Don't forget the birthday cake and candles. I did one year and I'm still reminded of it six years on.

SCORING THE GAMES

I'm all for a bit of healthy competition and, let's face it, children do like to compete. But this is a party and everyone wants to go home feeling like a winner, so try to keep it light-hearted and make sure that no one feels left out.

Use star charts or stickers as rewards. Draw up a simple grid and put a child's name in each square. Attach it to a wall with masking tape or blue tack. Stickers and stars go here after each game and are only added up at the end of the party. You can draw the stars onto the chart with brightly coloured felt pens or give the children stickers to attach themselves.

At one party I gave each child a piece of paper. They had to draw a picture on it so that they knew it was theirs. At the end of each game, they happily toddled off to put the stickers on their piece of paper. This gave me time to set the next game up.

To even things out don't just reward children for winning, also reward for skill, effort, patience, technique and silly things too like who laughed the most or who had the biggest grin. That way all the children have an equal chance of collecting rewards.

If you've got three or four children let them play the games as individuals. If there are more, use teams. Every member of the winning team gets a star or sticker as well as outstanding performers from the other team. Try mixing up the teams for each game as it avoids anyone feeling left out and all the children have an even chance of collecting rewards, not just the dexterous or sporty ones.

The rules for these games are really simple, so there's little room for argument on that front. In my experience, however, children are sticklers for justice and like to point out (as loudly as possible) cheating and other such misdemeanours. Make it clear that you make the rules so whatever you say goes and whatever decision you make, that is the end of the matter.

WHAT IF I HAVE ODD NUMBERS?

Easy Peasy.

For each game nominate one of the children to act as Umpire. Throughout the party each child will have a chance to take on this role. Their job is to say 'Ready, Steady, Go' and to nominate the winners at the end of the game.

I've tried this a few times and found that the kids leap at the chance to be in charge. Guess we all like an excuse to be bossy at times!

PRIZES

My personal view is that either no-one gets a prize or everyone does. It keeps it simple and there's no risk of tears and tantrums on the way home. As the stars or stickers are added up at the end of the game, there is no need to give out prizes during the party, unless you really want to.

If you've made sure that the stars and rewards have been fairly evenly distributed, when it gets to the end of the party you can say that everyone has done so well that everyone will get a little something to take home with them. It also helps to summarise who did well at what - making sure that every child did 'particularly well' at something.

As for the prizes, don't spend a fortune, keep it simple. It really is just a token. In my experience children don't care about the 'value' of things, just the fact that they've been given a prize is enough. If you are planning on handing out party bags, then make it clear that this is their 'prize' to take home. That's more than enough.

Ultimately you've got to do what you feel most comfortable with. Just because this is my way, it doesn't mean it's the right way.

BEFORE YOU START

These games are energetic so make sure there's plenty of water to drink.

Try not to give them chocolate, sweets or pop too early as noise volumes and energy levels tend to increase the more sugar they intake. Even the loveliest children can be hard work when they're sugared-up – especially in an exciting party environment.

Don't forget, the more children you have, the longer each game will take to play. And vice versa. If you're running out of time, skip a game. If you're speeding through the games, don't panic, there are some extra balloon games included, just in case. There's also a section on some good old fashioned favourites, like 'sausages', in case you want to include those.

Mix and match if you like. The point is to have fun so although the games are in a particular sequence, do them any way you like!

WHAT TO DO WITH PRESENTS

If this is just a two hour party then there's not really enough time to open presents in front of the guests. I'm sure they'd rather all play games. Instead nominate a room or table where the children can put their presents.

The birthday boy or girl can open the presents later.

Keep a pen handy and write the present that each child gave in the card that they sent. It's much easier to remember who to thank for what this way.

READY

STEADY

GO

CLOAKROOM CHAOS

This is a great warm-up game

Get the children to sit in a circle. Each child must take off their shoes and socks and put them in the middle of the circle. The children close their eyes while you mix up the pile of shoes and socks.

'Ready, steady go!' - the children have to race to find their own shoes and socks. The first to put them on is the winner. Also award 'merit' points or stars for things like neatly tied laces, least smelly shoes or coolest socks.

YOU CAN ALSO USE
Hats, gloves and scarves
Snorkels and flippers
Slippers and dressing gowns (great for a sleepover party)

TIP: You might want to use the invitation to specify that children wear shoes and socks for the party. Have some spares handy, just in case.

Don't forget you can use the invitation to get children to bring them along.

HOW TO ADAPT THIS GAME TO A THEMED PARTY
It's easy to make this game fit any theme. For example if yours is a Halloween party, get each child to draw a picture of a spider, a pumpkin and a witch's hat, put their name or initials on the picture and bring that along. Spread the pictures around the room making sure the children have their backs turned or eyes closed so they can't see where you're putting them. Then let them race to see who finds all their pictures first. Award extra stars for best spider or spookiest picture.

Younger children might struggle with buckles and laces, so this picture game is great for them as is hats and scarves or slippers and dressing gowns.

DISTRACTION
Terrible tongue twister ... who can say it three times in a row
"Peggy Babcock"
"Greek grapes" (for younger children)

STRAWS & PRETZELS

Separate the children into teams. Each team should form a line. Give each child a pretzel stick or straw that they put in their mouths (without munching if it's a pretzel!). The child at the front of each team is given a curly pretzel that they must pass to the next child using just the straw or stick in their mouth.

The first team to pass the pretzel down the line and back again wins the stars. If the pretzel or object is dropped it must go back to the person that dropped it ...if you want to make the game harder for older children ... back to the beginning of the line so they have to start again. Doh!

To make the game harder why not get each team to pass a selection of objects down the line to a bowl at the end. Set a time limit of say three minutes. Same rules as before. The team with the most objects when the whistle blows, wins.

For smaller groups of children, who want to play individually, get them to move a selection of objects from one side of the room to another, using just the straw. Whoever moves all their objects first, wins this game.

You can also award stars for the person who concentrated the hardest, pulled the best face or the one who managed to drop the prop the least amount of times.

YOU CAN ALSO USE

Anything* that you can dangle from a straw or pretzel stick and pass down a line.
Try pasta shapes such as bows or curled bits of tagliatelle
Play jewellery such as rings or bangles.
A piece of string or ribbon tied into a loop
Old curtain hooks
Make lightweight rings out of newspaper and sticky tape
* Be sensible about the type of prop you use with smaller children – make sure it's not going to be easily swallowed!

HOW TO ADAPT THIS GAME TO A THEMED PARTY

Just use objects that link to your party theme such as string lassos for a cowboy theme or cardboard stars with a loop at the top for a space-themed party.

Remember - If you have odd numbers nominate one child as umpire – they get to be bossy for this game. Best of all they get to say 'Ready, steady, go!' as well as nominate the winners.

DISTRACTION

One minute to go. The children have to move from one end of a room to another in one minute. Get one of the children to time the race and see who performs the task in as close to one minute as possible.

If they're not all chewed up, the children can use the same straws as earlier. If not give them a fresh one each. The idea of this game is to move stuff – like popcorn - from one bowl to another just using the straw. You can hold the straw but you have to move the object with the power of your puff. Explain to the children that they have to suck not blow! For younger children, give them all a chance to practise before the game begins.

As a team game, get one child to move one piece of popcorn, then run back to tag the next person, who does the same. As individuals it's just a race against time. The team or individual with the most pieces of popcorn wins. You can also award stars for the person who tried hardest and the person with the most interesting technique.

If you have an umpire, let them be in charge of counting the pieces.

You must use something that is at least twice the size of the hole in the straw because you don't want the children to accidentally suck it into their mouths. That could be dangerous. I use popcorn because it's cheap, easy to make and the pieces are big and light so easy to move using the straw. I remove all the small pieces before starting the game.

YOU CAN ALSO USE
Newspaper cut into strips or screwed up into small balls.
Chocolate buttons or other large light chocolates (you run the risk of sugared up kids if you use chocolates though!!)
Light crisps or snacks like rice crackers or prawn crackers

HOW TO ADAPT THIS GAME TO A THEMED PARTY
Use pictures on square pieces of paper (about 5cm squared) that the children have to move. If it's a fairy party, photocopy or draw pictures of little fairies wings, flowers etc. If it's a cowboy party go for pictures of horses, cowboy boots and baked beans.

DISTRACTION
Who can stand on one leg for the longest?

SQUEEZY CHEESE & CRACKERS

For this game the children have to build a tower using crackers and cheese spread. Start the game by placing a cracker on a plate for each team or individual child. (To cut down on mess from crumbs use a plastic tray or tea-towel underneath the plate so that you can quickly whip everything away at the end of the game.)

Ready, steady, go ... use a blob of squeezy cheese from a tube followed by a cracker and so on to build the tower.

For teams, make it a relay race so they run to the tower, add the cheese spread and cracker, run back to base and tag the next child, who does the same. If the tower tumbles the children can rebuild it. The game ends when one team or individual has used up all their crackers.

Stars go to the tallest tower, the neatest tower and the one you'd most like to eat. If you have an umpire – let them do the judging!

Unless they're really grubby and disgusting put the towers on the party table and the children can nibble them a little later.

YOU CAN ALSO USE

Any biscuit or cracker. Use smaller ones to make it more difficult for older children.
Toast some sliced bread and cut each slice into quarters
Try icing as the sticky stuff.
Salad cream or honey in a squeezy bottle is great fun but quite messy!

Tip: It's easier if the sticky stuff is in a tube or squeezy bottle but the children can always use a small teaspoon to apply it.

HOW TO ADAPT THIS GAME TO A THEMED PARTY

For Halloween you can use tomato puree from a tube as bat's blood.

DISTRACTION

Can the children pat their heads with one hand and make circles over their tummy with the other hand... at the same time!!

CHOPSTICKS

A variation on the game 'more straws', except that this time the children have to move the objects from one bowl to another, using just a pair of chopsticks. For a team game one child moves one object, then runs back and tags the next until time is up. For individuals it's simply a race against time.

For younger children use a pair or forks or spoons as they're a bit easier to control.

YOU CAN ALSO USE
Carrots chopped into chunks
Popcorn
Small light toys
Newspaper rolled into balls

HOW TO ADAPT THIS GAME TO A THEMED PARTY
You can use small plastic creepy crawlies for a Halloween party or, for a cowboy party, you could spray the popcorn with gold craft paint and pretend that it's golden nuggets.

COMFORT BREAK

Make sure there's plenty of water available rather than juice or pop.

TOP TIP
If you are using paper cups get the children to write their name or put a small picture on it, like a cat or big yellow sunshine, so that they know which one is theirs. Use blank computer labels or strips of paper stuck on with sticky tape for plastic cups.

Well done... you're almost half way through. Keep up the good work.

FANCY FOOTWORK

The children can keep their shoes and socks on for this one but if there's no risk of splinters from the floor it's better with bare feet.

The children have to lift various objects, like rolled up pairs of socks, from the floor and put them in an empty box, bucket or bowl ... using only their feet. They can only move one object at a time.

If the children are playing as individuals have 6 to 10 objects for them to move (depending on age). The first one to complete the task wins. If you have time, get them to do it again and see who's quickest out of three rounds.

For teams keep to around 5 or 6 objects. The first child in the team puts the objects in the bucket using their feet. Once all the objects are in the bucket they have to empty them back out onto the floor and run back to tag the next person. It makes sense to tip the objects out carefully because the next person can only use their feet, so the nearer they are to the bucket, the better. First team to finish the task wins. If it's just small teams, the game can end when everyone on the team has had two goes each.

Award extra stars for good technique (both filling the bucket and emptying it) and the person who giggled the most.

YOU CAN ALSO USE

Any fruit or veg that won't get too squishy like apples, pears, potatoes
Any balls such as tennis balls, ping pong balls, bean bags
Sheets of newspaper rolled into a ball
Pine cones
Small toys
Mix and match a selection of objects

HOW TO ADAPT THIS GAME TO A THEMED PARTY

For a fairy party it could be the ingredients for a magic spell like a cup to mix the potion in, an apple for a sweet wish and box of surprises (use a small box from a jewellers or wrap a small box in pretty paper).

DISTRACTION

Here's another terrible tongue-twister to try:
"Unique New York"
"Red Leather Yellow Leather"

LEMON RELAY
OR 'SOCK' RELAY OR 'ANYTHING' RELAY!

The aim of this game is to move a small object, like a lemon or rolled up socks, weaving it in and out between objects on an obstacle course. The thing is the children can only touch it with a stick (or chopstick, large serving spoon etc).

Use small teddies, cushions, upturned cups and buckets to mark out the obstacle course. For individuals let them take it in turns, time them and see who completes the whole course in the quickest time.

For teams each team member has to complete the course before tagging the next. The first team to finish wins.

Award extra stars for style, control and panache.

YOU CAN ALSO USE
Anything that can easily be rolled like balls, apples, potatoes, hard boiled eggs.
You can also make balls using newspaper screwed tightly and fastened with sticky tape.

HOW TO ADAPT THIS GAME TO A THEMED PARTY
For a Halloween party the children have to pit their wits against some ugly mugs. Tie balloons to mugs and decorate them with silly faces. You can use any props or pictures as part of the obstacle course. Perhaps fairies even have to complete the obstacle course in order to release the fairy princess from a wicked spell?

TIME FOR FOOD

If you are indoors make the children sit at a table... it keeps the mess in one place. Alternatively have a picnic on the floor with the children sitting in a circle.

Try not to bring out the sweet stuff until they've eaten some of the savoury!

Aim for around 20 minutes.

Remember that the children are excited about being at a party so all may not go according plan. Chances are that they're not as hungry as you might expect... this is often the case with younger children. Some of them may only want to nibble (no matter how delicious the food) and could get restless quite quickly. Don't be disappointed if they only sit down for 10 minutes!

Bring in the birthday cake when they start to get restless.

HAPPY BIRTHDAY TO YOU!

Get the children to help clear away some of the mess while you cut the cake. As an incentive, tell them that there'll be more games once everything's cleared away.

Just think... not long to go now.

WIND DOWN GAMES

Keep an eye on the time. At this point you could have anything between 10 to 30 minutes left. Allow around 10 to 15 minutes for 'pass the parcel with forfeits'.

There are enough balloon games here to keep the children entertained for up to half an hour. Don't forget there are some of the old-fashioned favourites like 'sausages', 'that chocolate game' and 'musical chairs' if you prefer.

BALLOON GAMES

AIR BALLOONS

See who can keep their balloon in the air the longest. As soon as someone lets their balloon fall to the ground, they're out of the game. If they look too good at this game change the rules after a couple of minutes so that they can only touch the balloon with their heads. Get older children to swap their balloon for one of another colour while all the balloons are still in the air.

If you're running out of time or the game is going on too long, declare any remaining children the winners.

POPTASTIC FUN

Option 1
Tie a piece of string to the end of a balloon. Each child has a balloon tied loosely to their ankles. The children have to try and pop everyone else's balloon using their feet (with socks on) or a with a piece of rolled-up newspaper. Whoever is left with an un-popped balloon wins the game.

Option 2
In pairs the children have to stand back to back with a balloon between them. See which pair can burst their balloon first.

Option 3
Have a box full of balloons for each team or individual. Arrange them at different ends of the room. Whichever team or individual pops all their balloons first wins.

Some children don't like the sound of popping balloons so avoid the noisy games if that's the case.

PASS THE PARCEL WITH FORFEITS

This is perfect as an end game as the children all sit down in a circle.

Simply wrap a gift in coloured paper then keep adding layers of paper (use newspaper because you can stick it in the recycling bag afterwards). With each layer add a small piece of paper with a forfeit, written on it. Make sure there are enough layers for each child at the party.

Sit the children in a circle, give the parcel to the birthday boy or girl. Put on some music and the parcel is passed around the circle. When the music stops, the child holding the parcel unwraps a layer and performs their forfeit. Continue, making sure that each child unwraps a layer, until there's just the prize left to unwrap. (I turn my back at this point so that I have no idea who will get the prize when I stop the music).

IDEAS FOR FORFEITS

Do an impression of a monkey

Quack like a duck, snort like a piglet, slither like a snake, wiggle like a worm etc

Pull the silliest face you can

Turn to the person on your right and say 'Three free throws' three times as quickly as you can

Do an impression of a teacher you all know and see if your friends can guess who it is.

Can you touch your nose with your toes?

Do 6 star jumps

Tell your friends the daftest thing you've ever done.

Yawn as loudly as possible (see if it makes anyone else yawn)

Turn to the person on your left and blow a raspberry.

Make up a sentence using the first letter of your name as many times as possible: For example "Tracey Turned to Toby and Told him a Terrible Tongue Twister"

OLD-FASHIONED FAVOURITES

You can't have a book on party games without including some of the good old-fashioned favourites.

MUSICAL CHAIRS

Make sure that there are as many chairs as there are children. Play some music, when the music stops everyone has to find a chair to sit on. That was just a practice run! After that you're going to take a chair away so that when the music stops, there is one child without a chair. That person is out. Take away another chair and continue until there are two children and one chair. The one that gets the chair is the winner. Make it clear that children who push and shove or play roughly will be disqualified. Get the children that are 'out' to help you spot this and to say who's out. Instead of chairs you can use cushions or pictures to suit your theme. For example, you could have pictures of spiders and other creepy creatures dotted around the room for a Halloween party. To make it funny you can have dressing up hats (or oversized clothes and shoes) and whoever is without a hat when the music stops is out.

STATUES

The same principle as musical chairs except that this time when the music stops everyone has to stand as still as statues. The first to move is out. Whoever is out can help you spot movements throughout the game so they are still part of the fun. To make it harder for the children, you can try to make them laugh by pulling funny faces or singing silly songs. Why not make up your own rules to make it even sillier?

THAT CHOCOLATE GAME

Whenever you mention party games to grown-ups they always say "Do you remember that chocolate game? It was my favourite". I'd advise playing this game towards the end of the party as it involves sugar! Children sit in a circle. In the middle there's a bar of chocolate, on a tray or large plate, with a knife and fork. Also in the circle is a hat, scarf and pair of gloves. The birthday boy or girl is handed a dice and the game begins. Each child rolls the dice in turn. When someone rolls a 6, they have to put on the hat, scarf and gloves then, using the knife and fork, they get to eat as much of the chocolate as they can. As soon as someone else rolls a 6 they have to stop, take off the hat, scarf and gloves and hand them to the next person to put on. Sometimes a child may only have got as far as putting on the hat, when the next child rolls a 6. Hey ho, that's the name of the game. All's fair in love and chocolate games. The game ends when the chocolate bar is finished (or sooner if you've had enough after 5 minutes!) Do look at the ingredients on the back of the chocolate bar and go for one with the highest percentage of cocoa solids. You can also try putting some chocolate buttons in the middle of the circle with a pair of chopsticks. For younger children only get them to put on a hat and scarf, just to make it a bit easier.

SAUSAGES

Best with a relatively small group of children, otherwise it could take ages. One child is nominated to answer questions from the other children. The only thing is that whatever the question, the only answer they are allowed to give is 'sausages'. The other children ask very silly questions to make them laugh. As soon as they do, it's someone else's turn to be asked questions.

NUTRITION ADVICE

It's really tempting to get carried away at parties and let the children have all the stuff they're not normally allowed. And why not? It does no harm if they usually eat pretty healthily. The thing is, many foods aimed at children contain additives, and one of the greatest concerns about additives is the effect of mixing them together. Some children are more chemically sensitive than others to things like additives, colourings, sugars and sweeteners, so much so that it can dramatically affect behaviour and lead to wild mood swings, hyperactivity and aggressive behaviour such as kicking and biting. With a room full of giddy children, this chemical cocktail could you leave you tearing your hair out.

WHERE DO YOU FIND THESE ADDITIVES?

Most fizzy pops and squashes contain colours, preservatives, sugar and artificial sweeteners. A pretty lethal combination if you ask me.

Almost all coloured sweets will be artificially coloured and full of sugar.

Most flavoured snack items will contain artificial colours, flavours and often MSG (E621) flavour enhancer.

Get into the habit of checking the label. As a general guide, the shorter the list of ingredients, the fewer the additives. Shop around.

THE IDEAL DIET

I know you've heard this before but the ideal diet should be full of fresh and unprocessed foods that are low in salt and sugar. This means eating as many vegetables, fruits, whole grains, pulses, beans and fish as possible, plus moderate amounts of dairy, meat and essential fats. When choosing fruit and vegetables, aim for seasonal organic choices where possible. A variety of different colours will provide the best mix of nutrients, especially black, red, orange and green fruits and vegetables.

Educating children from an early age about health and nutrition will help them to make good choices. As they get older they have an increasing amount of freedom over food choice and often eat outside the home. Outside factors such as peer pressure and advertising also start to play their part.

The best advice is to eat really well at home and allow a few deviations and treats when out. If 75% of the diet is optimum they will survive the rest.

RECIPES

Cooking is a life skill. Children who are given the opportunity to help in the kitchen tend to be less fussy about food. By making their own treats, children can learn what goes in them and you can control the quality of the ingredients.

The brief I gave to Hazel was: simple food that is easy to prepare and doesn't cost a fortune. It also has to be healthy and delicious. Food that kids actually want to eat... even the fussy ones. I've tested out these recipes on various children to resounding success. According to them this food is 'yum yum' and definitely not 'yuck yuck'.

All the food pictured in this book was made by me, in my small, ill-equipped kitchen. I haven't used stylists or professional caterers for the photographs because I wanted to show real food prepared by someone who is not particularly accomplished in the culinary department.

Everything here can be made the night before and kept in the fridge. There are some 'hot' food options, but this is only practical if someone else is in charge of the oven, while you entertain the kids.

For your buffet, aim for a variety of different grains, fruits, vegetables and protein foods. Provide vegetarian choices and be aware of food allergies and intolerances. For this reason it is best to avoid nuts when catering for other children.

Drinking water is a good habit to get your children into and will be made easier if offered from an early age. If thirsty, give them water first, not juice. If you use tap water, filter it and change the filter regularly to remove pollutants and chemicals. Dilute fruit and vegetable juices 50:50 with water.

STICKY SAUSAGE & SWEETCORN KEBABS

Makes approx 10
Can be eaten hot or cold.

1 tbs honey

1 tbs soy sauce

1 tsp olive oil

8 good quality pork sausages, each sliced into 4

2 small courgettes, thickly sliced

2 peppers (1 red and 1 yellow sliced into bite sized pieces)

16 baby sweetcorn

Thread the sausages and vegetables onto skewers. Mix the honey, soy sauce and olive oil together and brush all over.

Line your grill pan with foil and cook the kebabs under a medium grill for 15 minutes or until cooked through, turning frequently.

VEGGIE OPTION
Use haloumi instead of sausages

PIZZA PINWHEELS

Makes 12
Can be eaten hot or cold.

375g/15oz pack ready puff pastry, thawed if frozen

6 tbs home-made pasta sauce* or tomato puree
(or good quality ready-made pasta sauce)

100g/4oz wafer thin ham (check no additives)

75g /3oz spinach

100g/4oz Cheddar cheese, grated

1 free-range egg, beaten or milk

1 tsp dried oregano or mixed herbs

Heat oven to 200C/Gas 6.

Roll the pastry to 40 x 32cm. Spread a layer of pasta sauce over it.

Arrange the ham and/or spinach over the top then scatter with grated cheese.

Starting at one of the short ends, roll the pastry up as tightly as possible.
Chill in the fridge for approx 10mins.

Cut the roll into 12 equal slices and lay flat on baking trays. Brush lightly
with beaten egg or milk and sprinkle with herbs. Bake for 12-15 minutes until
puffed and golden.

VEGGIE OPTION
Omit the ham
* pasta sauce: 1 red onion chopped, 1 tin chopped tomatoes, 1 pepper chopped,
1 carrot grated, small courgette grated, olive oil for cooking. Fry the onion in
oil until soft, add the other ingredients and cook for 10 mins. Whizz to a puree.

SANDWICHES

Use granary or wholemeal bread or rolls. If you need to use white, buy a fresh loaf and ask for it to be sliced. Avoid sliced white bread, it has practically no nutritional value whatsoever. If necessary mix & match sandwiches with one slice brown, one slice white.

SAVOURY SANDWICHES

Marmite & cheese; egg mayonnaise & cress, ham & mango chutney; cress, watercress & grated carrot in mayonnaise; carrot, soft cheese & apricots.

SWEET SANDWICHES

Date spread (chop some dates and cook them gently in a small saucepan with a little water and the juice of half a lemon or orange. Beat to a smooth paste.); honey & oatmeal (bake a handful of fine oatmeal in the oven until light brown. Spread the bread with butter and honey and sprinkle with oatmeal); cottage cheese, pineapple & dates.

The date spread is a complete revelation. No only did it pass 'the fussiest eater I know' test with flying colours, I am so taken with it that I like to use it on my toast in a morning instead of jam.

PASTA SALADS

TUNA PASTA

You can't go far wrong with a Tuna Pasta Salad. It's simple and, if you're worried about fussy eaters, it's a pretty safe bet.

Cook 225g/8oz pasta (preferably wholemeal) following the directions on the back of the packet, add 1 tin of good quality drained tuna, 4 tbs mayonnaise and 1 stick of celery, finely chopped.

GREEK SALAD

If you want to try something a little more adventurous, but still fairly safe, what about this quick and easy version of a Greek Salad?

Cook 50g/2oz small pasta (I used organic alphabet shapes), add chopped olives, cucumber, cherry tomatoes and feta cheese. Stir together with 2 tbs red wine vinegar and 3 tbs olive oil.

CHEESY BISCUITS

Makes approx 20

75g/3oz spelt/wholemeal flour (or half wholemeal/half white)

50g/2oz butter

75g/3oz medium Cheddar cheese, grated

1 free-range egg, beaten

1tbs sesame seeds

Turn oven on to 190C/Gas 5.

Put the flour into a bowl, add the butter and rub in using your fingertips
(or use a food processor) until the mixture resembles fine breadcrumbs.

Stir in the cheese, then mix in the egg (leave 1 tbs) to make a smooth dough.

Gently knead the dough, then roll out on a lightly floured surface to a 5mm
(1/4 inch) thickness.

Cut into circles, numbers, letters or animal shapes.

Brush with remaining egg and sprinkle with sesame seeds.

Bake for 10 minutes, until golden.

Store in an airtight container and use within 1 week.

QUICK & EASY

A SIMPLE SELECTION OF BREAD STICKS, RICE CRACKERS, WEDGES OF HARD BOILED EGGS AND DIPS INCLUDING HUMMUS, SALSA AND GUACAMOLE.

Bits on Sticks: Cover a baking potato or grapefruit in foil and dot the cocktail sticks all over. Mix the protein, fruit and vegetables together on one cocktail stick to make it look appealing.

Protein: Chicken chunks, slices of ham rolled up, cheese (eg goat's, cheddar, feta), smoked salmon
Vegetables: Cherry tomatoes, cucumber, carrots, celery, red pepper, baby sweetcorn
Fruit: Apricots, kiwi, strawberries, red grapes, satsumas, mango, melon, pineapple

Home made Hummus:
1 tin chickpeas
1 lemon
1 clove garlic, crushed
approx 4 tbs extra virgin olive oil
cayenne pepper or Tabasco to taste
Blend together, adding extra water or oil if needed until preferred consistency. Will keep in the fridge for 5 days.

Mixture of dried fruits: Dates, dried apricots, apple, pear, banana chips

Fresh fruit dipped in chocolate: Strawberries are great.

POPCORN
Popcorn is a nutritious snack and is fun and easy to do with children.
2 tbs popcorn
1 tbs olive oil

Heat the oil in a saucepan until it just starts to smoke.
Add the popcorn and place the lid on the pan.
Turn the heat down. The corn will pop for about 5 minutes.
When the popping has stopped, remove from heat.
Have a quick check through and remove any corn that hasn't popped.

Sweet popcorn: Melt a knob of butter and add about 3 tbs maple syrup or honey. Stir into popcorn
Savoury popcorn: Add finely grated parmesan

PITTA POCKETS

Lightly toast the pitta bread, cut it in half and stuff with pesto, soft cheese & lettuce or tuna & sweetcorn mayonnaise (or any of the sandwich suggestions). Arrange standing up in a container.

QUESADILLA

Put a handful of grated cheese, finely sliced spring onions and finely chopped red peppers on a wholemeal tortilla. Place another tortilla on top and dry-fry them in a non-stick pan over a medium heat for a couple of minutes either side so the outside is crispy and the cheese has melted. Cut into triangles.

LITTLE CAKES
FOR LITTLE HANDS TO DECORATE

This would be the best size for young children who tend to take one mouthful, then leave the rest.

100g/4oz butter

100g/4oz castor sugar

75g/3oz self raising flour

25g/1oz cocoa powder, sieved

2 free-range eggs

12 paper cake cases

Turn oven on to 190C/Gas 5.

Using an electric beater, whisk the butter with the sugar until creamy. You can do this by hand but it does make your arm ache. Sieve the flour and the cocoa powder together in a separate bowl.

Add one egg and half the flour mixture, and whisk until combined. Add the second egg with the rest of the flour mix. It should drop off the spoon easily, if not add 1-2 tbs milk.

Place 12 paper cases in a 12-hole cake tin. Divide the mixture between the paper cases.

Bake for about 20 minutes, until risen and springy to touch. Cool on a wire rack.

Icing:
Make a water icing by sieving 150g (6oz) icing sugar into a bowl. Stir in about 1 tbs water and mix until a smooth icing is formed. Place a little icing on each cake and spread out to cover the tops.

To decorate:
Use cherries, sultanas, chocolate buttons, coconut etc to make your own decoration. Try to avoid anything with colourings.

CARROT MUFFINS

Dairy free option
Makes 12:

100g/4oz grated carrot

150ml/5fl oz olive oil

100g/4oz soft brown sugar

2 free-range eggs

225g/8oz plain flour, preferable Spelt or wholemeal

1 tsp baking powder

pinch of salt

1 tsp ground cinnamon

12 paper muffin cases

Turn oven on to 180C/Gas 4.

Peel & grate the carrots.

Put the oil, sugar and eggs in a bowl and beat together with a wooden spoon
or use an electric whisk or hand blender.

Sift the flour and baking powder into the mixture.

Add a pinch of salt and the cinnamon. Mix.

Fold in the grated carrots.

Put 12 paper cases in a muffin tin and divide the mixture between them.

Bake in the oven for 25 minutes until well risen and golden.

To decorate:
When they are cool, spread with a water icing. Sieve 175g (6oz) icing sugar into
a bowl. Stir in about 1 tbs water and mix until a smooth icing is formed. Put a
tiny bit of grated carrot on top of the icing to give it some colour.

If 'dairy' is acceptable make a cream cheese topping with 100g/4oz soft butter,
300g/12oz soft cream cheese, 150g/6oz icing sugar. Mix the butter and cheese
together, sieve the icing sugar into the mixture and combine. Add a drop of cold
water if mixture is too stiff.

RAISIN FLAPJACK

Dairy & wheat free
Makes 12-14 slices

300g/12oz raisins, washed and dried (preferably the large lexia raisins)
3 tbs honey
75ml/3fl oz extra-virgin olive oil
250g/9oz rolled oats
50g/2oz desiccated coconut

Turn the oven on to 180C/Gas 4.

Place the raisins in a pan with 150ml/5fl oz water and heat gently for about 10 minutes to soften them. Add the honey and stir then leave to cool for a few minutes.

Place the contents of the pan into a food processor and process briefly or use a hand blender. Stir in the olive oil, oats, coconut and mix well together.

Press this mixture into a 27 x 18cm (7 x 11") Swiss roll tin or round cake tin and gently press down.

Bake for about 20 minutes until lightly browned on top. Cool in the tin.

BIRTHDAY CAKE

If the rest of the spread is a healthy mix, then there is nothing better than a good old-fashioned chocolate cake.

To make 2 chocolate sponges (20cm/8" diameter) you need:

200g/8oz butter

200g/8oz castor sugar

150g/6oz self raising flour

50g/2oz cocoa powder, sieved

4 free-range eggs

Turn oven on to 190C/Gas 5.

Take the butter out of the fridge to soften. Using an electric beater, whisk the butter with the sugar until creamy. You can do this by hand but it does make your arm ache. Sieve the flour and the cocoa powder together in a separate bowl.

Add one egg and a portion of the flour mixture, and whisk until combined. Continue adding each egg with some flour until both have been incorporated.

The mixture should drop off the spoon easily, if not add 1-2 tbs milk. Divide the mixture between 2 greased cake tins.

Bake for 20-25 minutes until risen and springy to touch. Turn out onto a wire cooling rack.

CHOCOLATE BUTTER ICING

75g/3oz butter

3 tbs milk

25g/1oz cocoa powder, sieved

1 tsp vanilla essence

250g/9oz icing sugar

Melt butter with milk in a small saucepan. Blend in cocoa and vanilla essence.

Stir in icing sugar and beat until smooth.

Use half the mixture to sandwich the cakes together and spread the remaining icing on top. For a large gathering keep as 2 separate cakes.

COOL STUFF TO MAKE

INVITATIONS
ALL-IN-ONE

Using a small plate as a template cut out a circle from a piece of paper. Decorate one side leaving space in the middle to write the name of the person you want to invite.

Add the invitation information on the opposite side. With the invitation information facing up, fold the sides inwards so that you end up with an envelope and invite all in one.

Fasten the back with some sticky tape or use a colourful sticker.

Shiver Me Timbers

I Be 'Avin A Party

INVITATIONS

LOOK IT'S ME!

Use a photograph of the birthday child. If
you have a digital camera you can do
this on your computer. Or you can use an
old photograph and photocopy it, then
stick it onto card.

INVITATIONS

Or download this invitation for free from our website www.ziegel.co.uk

INVITATION INFORMATION

It's my party

At

Date

Time

Please bring with you

Please wear

My telephone number

Please let me know
if you can come

From

PARTY BAGS
BOTTLE BOTTOMS

Cut the bottom off an empty plastic milk bottle. Only paint the outside. Use acrylic paints or decorate with glitter, pictures, wrapping paper, ribbons etc. Use a hole punch and thread through string, ribbon or pipe-cleaners as handles.

PARTY BAGS
RECYCLED BAGS

You can get hold of plain brown or coloured recycled paper bags from the internet very cheaply. If you're on good terms with your local grocer or health food shop you can ask if they will sell you some of their supply. Decorate them using paints, coloured pencils, pens, glitter, tissue, ribbons etc.

For fun you can also attach name tags with wooden pegs.

PARTY BAGS

FUNNELS

Use a large dinner plate to draw a circle on some plain or coloured card, then fold in half and cut along the fold. Before you assemble decorate one side (this will be the outside) with coloured pens, pencils or paints. You can also use wrapping paper as decoration by sticking it on to the card.

To make a funnel bring the straight sides together until they overlap. Fasten with staples or sticky tape.

To stop things falling out, put some tissue paper over the top and fasten in place with some tape. A simple handle can be made with some string.

COOL STUFF FOR BAGS

Pots and seeds: You can get seeds, bulbs, small pots and small bags of compost from the local garden centre. Separate the seeds into small paper envelopes (make your own using paper or tin foil) and put enough compost to fill the pot into several small bags. Using the instructions from the back of the seed or bulb packet, make your own note to pop in the party bag so the children know how to plant them when they get home.

Air dry clay: Buy a big block from your local art shop, cut it into smaller pieces and wrap it in plastic so that it doesn't dry out. Make suggestions of things the children can make out of their clay like a small pot or something to hang on their wall. Give instructions on how long to leave it to dry and how to paint it. You'll find this information on the back of the packet of clay. Younger children will need supervision when using the clay.

Popcorn: Use one of the delicious recipes in the book (see page 75) and send the children home with their own bag of home-made popcorn. Simple, inexpensive and delicious.

Home-made butter biscuits: Pipe names or initials on them and pop them into your party bags.

Other ideas: Colouring pens, crayons and pencils will always go down well. I also found some interesting wooden toys in my local garden centre.

HAZEL'S MUM'S EASY-SQUEEZY BUTTER BISCUITS

9oz plain flour

6oz softened butter

3 oz sugar

These are so simple to make. Put all the ingredients in a bowl and keep squeezing everything together with your hands until you have a ball of dough. Roll out onto a floured surface until about $1/2$cm thick. Cut into shapes with a cookie cutter.

Place on a greased baking tray and bake at 190°C for 10 minutes.

GREAT PARTIES DON'T HAVE TO BE COMPLICATED OR EXPENSIVE

INDEX

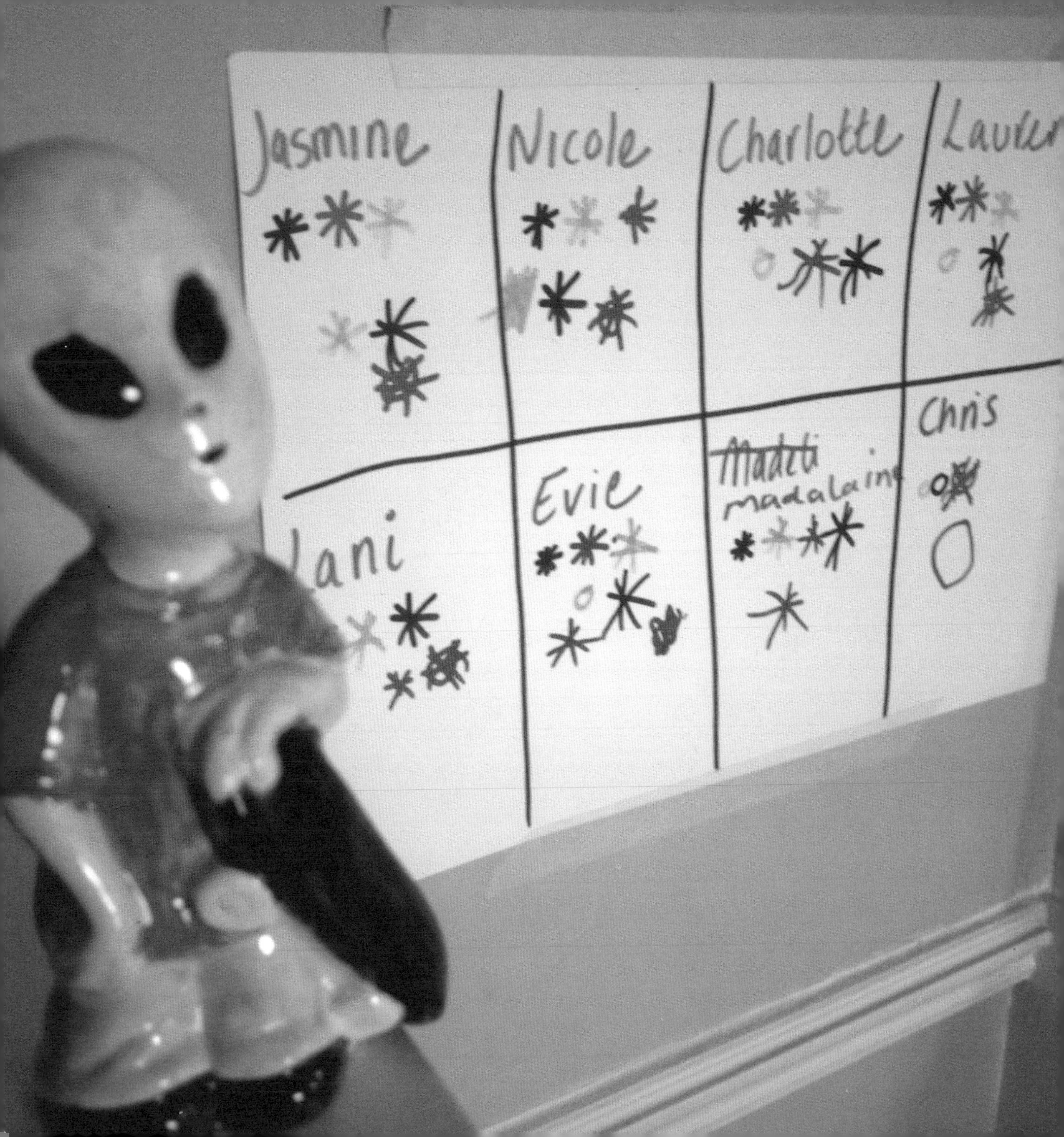
Jasmine
Nicole
Charlotte
Evie
Madeli
madalaine
Chris

ACKNOWLEDGMENTS

Ellie, you've been my number 1 guinea pig and my number 1 girl. Thank you for being wise beyond your years and for not getting cross with mummy on her 'stressy' days. I am blessed to have you in my life.

Chris, your endless supply of enthusiasm and creativity has helped turn my dream into a reality. I am so proud of this book, you've worked hard and done a superb job, thank you.

Hazel, it was a tall order, but you came up trumps. My life has changed since I discovered your delicious date spread and the easy squeezy butter biscuits. Yum!

Marianne and Carolyn, I am so lucky to have such clever and helpful friends. Thank you for listening patiently, dispensing wisdom wisely and lending me your children frequently.

Sarah, my head sits firmly on my shoulders thanks to you!

Sandra and Mary Lu, thank you for spotting the gaffs, gaps and gaping errors.

To all the children appearing in this book. What a joy it was to play my games with you. Thank you for letting us take pictures: Archie, Beth, Charlotte, Cherelle, Edie, Ellie, Evie, George, Hannah, Heather, Indie, Jackson, Jasmine, John, Jonothan, Lachan, Lani, Lauren, Lucy, Maddi, Martha, Milly, Nicole, Olivia, Oscar, Scarlett, Thomas.

A final, rather enormous thank you goes to the many children over the years that have been game enough to try out my silly ideas. Without them this book would simply never have happened.

Lani Cloke (seven)